AF574797

Welcome!

Are you ready to get your trilogy up and running?

No matter where you're starting from, planning a novel (or three) is a simple process... if you have a process.

Without a process it's *hard*.

Simple doesn't necessarily mean easy though - you still need to come up with story ideas and put them together. This workbook provides the process and space to get it all in order.

All you need to do is fill in the blanks. Simple, if not easy.

Inside you'll find a trilogy-overview section and three novel templates.

Once you've filled in the blanks you'll have a complete outline that's comprehensive enough to cover all the story bases you need to write your trilogy, with enough space left over for plenty of creativity.

When you're done planning, use it as your 'once source of truth' reference book.

Good luck with your epic masterpiece!

Your opinion matters to me!

Please let me know what you think of this workbook by leaving a review where you purchased it.

If you have any improvements you'd like to see, email your ideas to Chris@ChrisAndrews.me

Enjoy!

Chris

Using This Workbook

This workbook is a companion to *Character and Structure,* which delivers all the core knowledge professional storytellers use for developing and troubleshooting stories, and shows you how to use it.

You don't have to have read *Character and Structure* to use this workbook, but you'll certainly get more from it if you have.

If you already have a solid understanding of storytelling, you're good to go. If not, you can get clarity on any terms you're uncertain about through a simple internet search.

This workbook is easy enough for anyone with a basic grasp of storytelling to utilise it, yet in-depth enough to provide everything you need to outline a complex story over three books.

Although this workbook is based around a simple process, you don't have to be a slave to it. Feel free to repurpose anything you like. It's your workbook, after all.

It's also a handy place to keep your ideas together, and it makes for a great teaching aid.

That's it. It's now time to get started.

Simply fill in the blanks and you'll have everything you need to hit all the major story points necessary for writing your novel, with plenty of room for additional scenes, chapters, dialogue snippets, and notes.

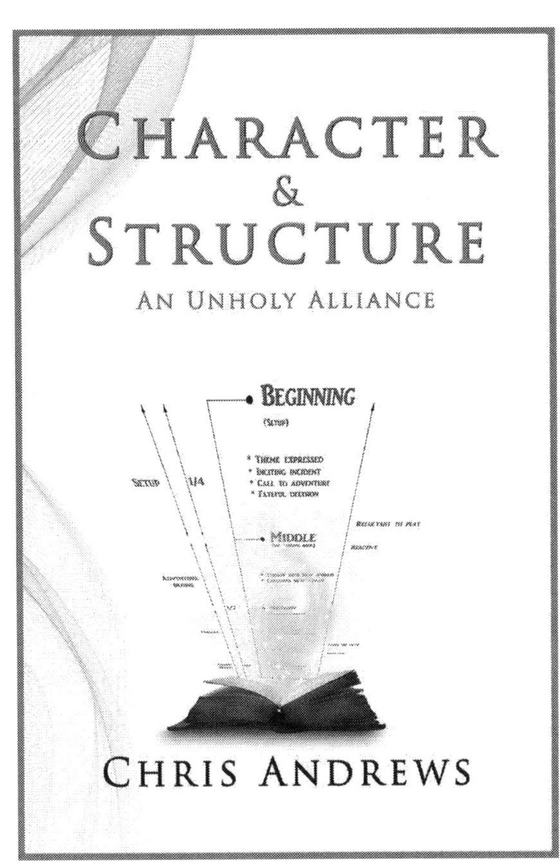

Assumptions

Although storytelling is based on your own assumed knowledge and your audience's expectations, meaning they're all alike in many ways, stories differ in focus, genre, length, number of chapters and scenes etc. Trilogies differ even more.

Because of that I've had to make some assumptions. To accommodate those assumptions and add flexibility, I've added extra sections with indicative headings you can use in any way you like.

Assumption 1. Your trilogy utilises an overarching storyline – the three books, even if they stand alone, tell a single story.

Assumption 2. Each novel in your trilogy is perfectly balanced in terms of the number of chapters per quarter (a stupid assumption, but we have to start somewhere). While the length of each section needs to be about the same for a well-balanced story, the number of chapters and scenes can vary drastically across books.

Assumption 3. Your novels are going to have exactly 40 chapters – 10 per quarter (the numbers work really well, but there's room for extra chapters if you need more). 40 chapters at 2000-3000 words per chapter makes your novels 80,000-120,000 words each in total. That's approximately what publishers look for. Feel free to adjust that in any way you like.

Assumption 4. You already have a reasonable grasp of storytelling from reading *Character and Structure: An Unholy Alliance* or through your own research. Because of that assumed knowledge the terms used within aren't explained in depth, but it's not hard to look them up.

Good luck! I'm looking forward to hearing about your success!

Novel Structure Diagram

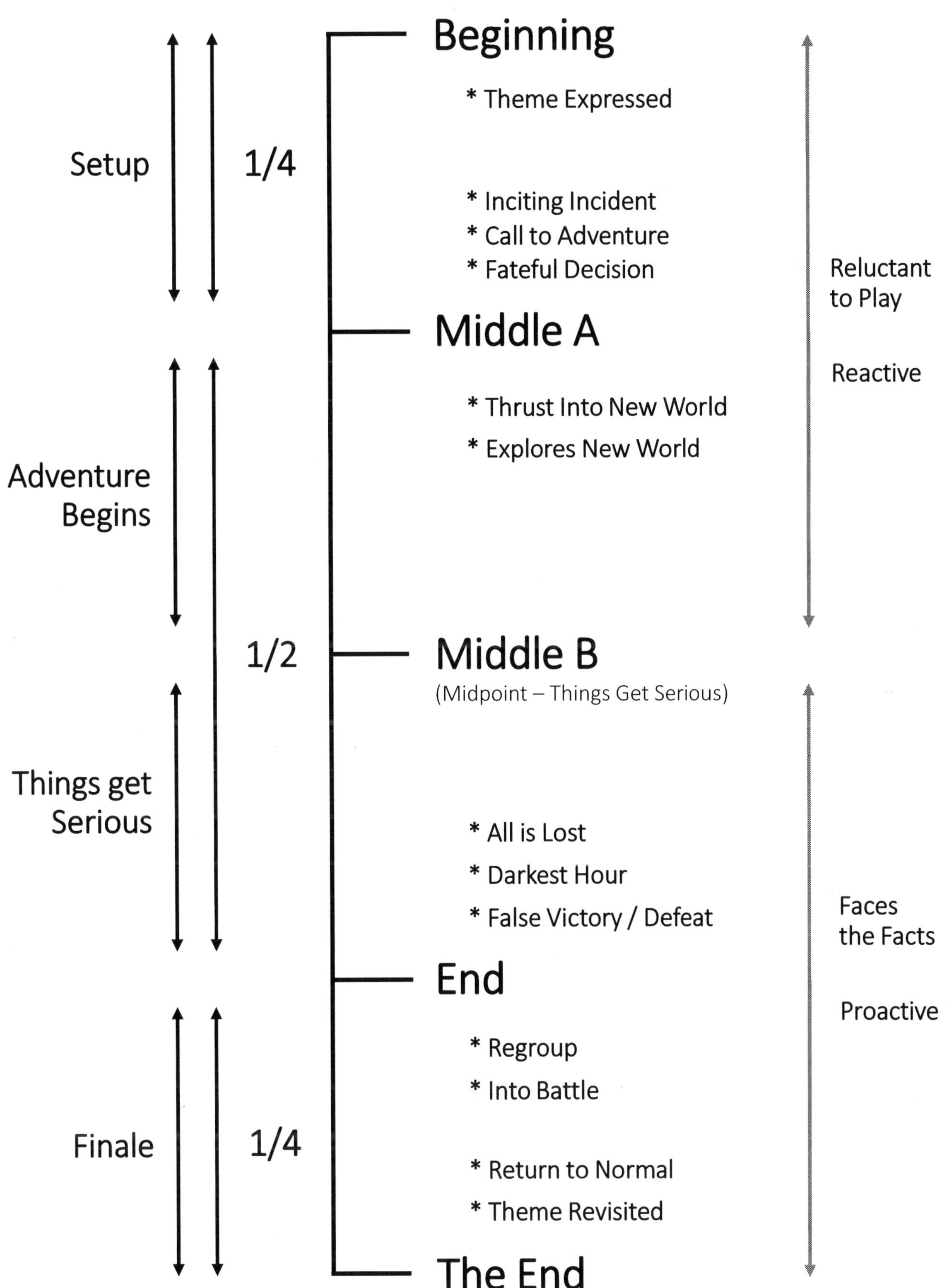

Trilogy Structure Diagram

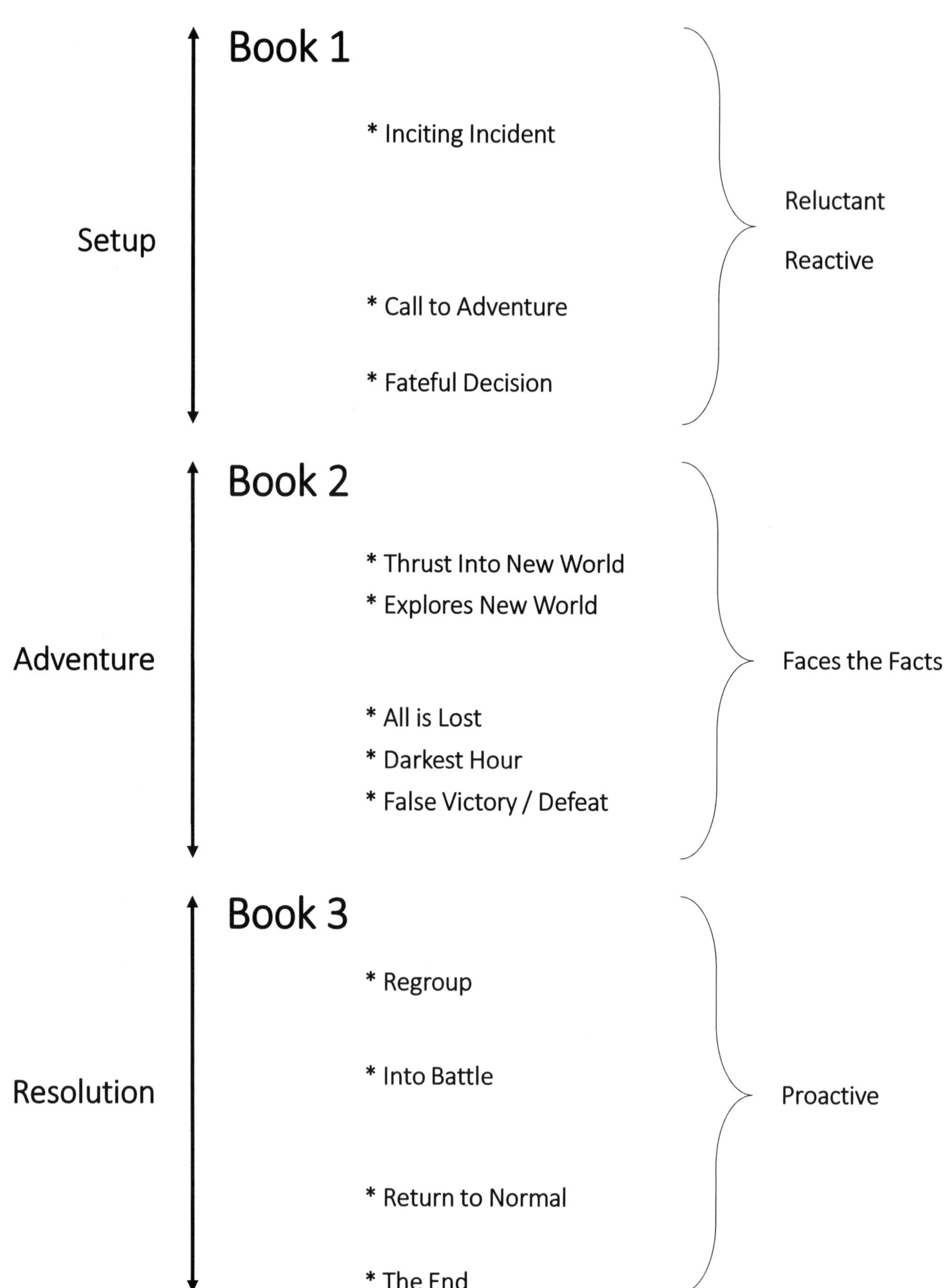

Example: Trilogy Breakdown

'Book' 1:	**A naïve Farm Boy must get the stolen plans for a super weapon to a rebel stronghold.**
Inciting Incident:	Rebels have stolen the secret plans for the super weapon, and the plans fall into the hands of a Farm Boy.
Call to Adventure:	Farm Boy is asked to help get the secret plans to the rebellion
Fateful Decision:	The reluctant Farm Boy decides to get the plans to the Princess who leads the rebellion. He succeeds, and uses the plans to destroy the super weapon.
'Book' 2:	**A gifted Farm Boy must learn magic and swordplay to defeat an Evil Overlord's Minion and save his friends.**
Thrust into New World:	Evil Overlord's forces attack. Farm Boy is thrust into battle.
Explores New World:	Following the battle, Farm Boy seeks Magic Teacher while friends flee the Evil Overlord's forces.
All is Lost:	Farm Boy's friends are captured by the Evil Overlord's Minion. Farm Boy loses fight with Minion.
Darkest Hour:	Minion reveals he's Farm Boy's Dad and wants to recruit him and take over the galaxy! Friends are lost. Farm Boy would rather die than join Dad.
False Victory / Defeat:	Friends save Farm Boy, but one friend has been captured and the rebellion is in disarray.
'Book' 3:	**A newly-minted Hero (former Farm Boy) must defeat the Evil Overlord and help destroy a new and more powerful super weapon.**
Regroup:	After saving his friend, the Farm Boy and friends and allies regroup to take on the Evil Overlord's bigger, better super weapon.
Into Battle:	They have a plan: sneak in and destroy the super weapon's defences to let the fleet attack the Evil Overlord's super weapon. Hero tries to save Dad's soul and succeeds on all counts.
Return to Normal:	Big party and celebrations ensue in a safer galaxy.

Trilogy Overview

Trilogy Name:

Overarching storyline:
Describe the overarching story across all three books

Notes

Overarching Story - Breakdown

Book 1:
Inciting Incident:
Call to Adventure:
Fateful Decision:

Overarching Story - Breakdown

Book 2:
Thrust into New World:
Explores New World:
All is Lost:
Darkest Hour:
False Victory / Defeat:

Overarching Story - Breakdown

Book 3:
Regroup:
Into Battle:
Return to Normal:

Primary Characters

Describe your characters so people will care about them

Name: Details:	Name: Details:
Name: Details:	Name: Details:
Name: Details:	Name: Details:
Name: Details:	Name: Details:
Name: Details:	Name: Details:
Name: Details:	Name: Details:

Novel 1

Title:
Subtitle:
Story overview / blurb:

Details

Genre:
Story Premise: (25 Words of Less)
Primary Theme:
First Half: (What happens?) What problems will be raised? What questions will be raised?
Second Half: (What happens?) How will you resolve these problems? How will you answer these questions? Unresolved problems or questions for sequels?

Story Overview

First Quarter Setup
Second Quarter Adventure Begins
Third Quarter Things Get Serious
Fourth Quarter Resolution

Storylines

Primary Storyline: Introduction: Resolution: How it contributes to Primary storyline:
Subplot 1 (i.e., Romance) Introduction: Resolution: How it contributes to Primary storyline:
Subplot 2 Introduction: Resolution: How it contributes to Primary storyline:
Subplot 3 Introduction: Resolution: How it contributes to Primary storyline:
Subplot 4 Introduction: Resolution: How it contributes to Primary storyline:

Character Meets Structure

Hook/opening:
Theme expressed:
Call to Adventure:
Fateful Decision:
Thrust into New World:
Explores New World:
All Is Lost:
Darkest Hour:
False Victory/Defeat:
Regroup:
Into Battle:
Return to Normal:
Theme Revisited:

Beginning – Chapter Overview

Chapter 1:
Chapter 2:
Chapter 3:
Chapter 4:
Chapter 5:
Chapter 6:
Chapter 7:
Chapter 8:
Chapter 9:
Chapter 10:

Middle (A) - Chapter Overview

Chapter 11:
Chapter 12:
Chapter 13:
Chapter 14:
Chapter 15:
Chapter 16:
Chapter 17:
Chapter 18:
Chapter 19:
Chapter 20:

Middle (B) - Chapter Overview

Chapter 21:
Chapter 22:
Chapter 23:
Chapter 24:
Chapter 25:
Chapter 26:
Chapter 27:
Chapter 28:
Chapter 29:
Chapter 30:

The End – Chapter Overview

Chapter 31:
Chapter 32:
Chapter 33:
Chapter 34:
Chapter 35:
Chapter 36:
Chapter 37:
Chapter 38:
Chapter 39:
Chapter 40:

Scene Ideas or Extra Chapters

Scene Ideas or Extra Chapters

Dialogue Ideas

Notes

Notes

Novel 2

Title:
Subtitle:
Story overview / blurb:

Details

Genre:

Story Premise:
(25 Words of Less)

Primary Theme:

First Half:
(What happens?)

What problems
will be raised?

What questions
will be raised?

Second Half:
(What happens?)

How will you resolve
these problems?

How will you answer
these questions?

Unresolved problems
or questions for sequels?

Story Overview

First Quarter
Setup

Second Quarter
Adventure Begins

Third Quarter
Things Get Serious

Fourth Quarter
Resolution

Storylines

Primary Storyline:

Introduction:

Resolution:

How it contributes to Primary storyline:

Subplot 1 (i.e., Romance)

Introduction:

Resolution:

How it contributes to Primary storyline:

Subplot 2

Introduction:

Resolution:

How it contributes to Primary storyline:

Subplot 3

Introduction:

Resolution:

How it contributes to Primary storyline:

Subplot 4

Introduction:

Resolution:

How it contributes to Primary storyline:

Character Meets Structure

Hook/opening:
Theme expressed:
Call to Adventure:
Fateful Decision:
Thrust into New World:
Explores New World:
All Is Lost:
Darkest Hour:
False Victory/Defeat:
Regroup:
Into Battle:
Return to Normal:
Theme Revisited:

Beginning – Chapter Overview

Chapter 1:
Chapter 2:
Chapter 3:
Chapter 4:
Chapter 5:
Chapter 6:
Chapter 7:
Chapter 8:
Chapter 9:
Chapter 10:

Middle (A) - Chapter Overview

Chapter 11:
Chapter 12:
Chapter 13:
Chapter 14:
Chapter 15:
Chapter 16:
Chapter 17:
Chapter 18:
Chapter 19:
Chapter 20:

Middle (B) - Chapter Overview

Chapter 21:
Chapter 22:
Chapter 23:
Chapter 24:
Chapter 25:
Chapter 26:
Chapter 27:
Chapter 28:
Chapter 29:
Chapter 30:

The End – Chapter Overview

Chapter 31:
Chapter 32:
Chapter 33:
Chapter 34:
Chapter 35:
Chapter 36:
Chapter 37:
Chapter 38:
Chapter 39:
Chapter 40:

Scene Ideas or Extra Chapters

Scene Ideas or Extra Chapters

Dialogue Ideas

Notes

Notes

Novel 3

Title:

Subtitle:

Story overview / blurb:

Details

Genre:
Story Premise: (25 Words of Less)
Primary Theme:
First Half: (What happens?) What problems will be raised? What questions will be raised?
Second Half: (What happens?) How will you resolve these problems? How will you answer these questions? Unresolved problems or questions for sequels?

Story Overview

First Quarter Setup
Second Quarter Adventure Begins
Third Quarter Things Get Serious
Fourth Quarter Resolution

Storylines

Primary Storyline:

Introduction:

Resolution:

How it contributes to Primary storyline:

Subplot 1 (i.e., Romance)

Introduction:

Resolution:

How it contributes to Primary storyline:

Subplot 2

Introduction:

Resolution:

How it contributes to Primary storyline:

Subplot 3

Introduction:

Resolution:

How it contributes to Primary storyline:

Subplot 4

Introduction:

Resolution:

How it contributes to Primary storyline:

Character Meets Structure

Hook/opening:
Theme expressed:
Call to Adventure:
Fateful Decision:
Thrust into New World:
Explores New World:
All Is Lost:
Darkest Hour:
False Victory/Defeat:
Regroup:
Into Battle:
Return to Normal:
Theme Revisited:

Beginning – Chapter Overview

Chapter 1:
Chapter 2:
Chapter 3:
Chapter 4:
Chapter 5:
Chapter 6:
Chapter 7:
Chapter 8:
Chapter 9:
Chapter 10:

Middle (A) - Chapter Overview

Chapter 11:
Chapter 12:
Chapter 13:
Chapter 14:
Chapter 15:
Chapter 16:
Chapter 17:
Chapter 18:
Chapter 19:
Chapter 20:

Middle (B) - Chapter Overview

Chapter 21:
Chapter 22:
Chapter 23:
Chapter 24:
Chapter 25:
Chapter 26:
Chapter 27:
Chapter 28:
Chapter 29:
Chapter 30:

The End – Chapter Overview

Chapter 31:
Chapter 32:
Chapter 33:
Chapter 34:
Chapter 35:
Chapter 36:
Chapter 37:
Chapter 38:
Chapter 39:
Chapter 40:

Scene Ideas or Extra Chapters

Scene Ideas or Extra Chapters

Dialogue Ideas

Notes

Notes

Notes

If you found this workbook helpful, I would consider it a huge favour if you left a review wherever you purchased it.

Thank you, in advance.

Chris

The Workbooks & Writer's Diary

www.chrisandrews.me/workbooks

Stay in Touch

If you'd like to stay in touch, you can keep up to date with my projects and subscribe to my newsletter via my website:

- http://www.chrisandrews.me

Wishing you the best of luck and success,

Chris Andrews

Made in the USA
Monee, IL
07 July 2026

56544783R00033